HOW TO WRITE A

BESTSELLING MEMOIR

Three Steps to Success

Victoria Twead

New York Times and Wall Street Journal bestselling author of

Chickens, Mules and Two Old Fools

Two Old Fools ~ Olé

Two Old Fools on a Camel

Two Old Fools in Spain Again

One Young Fool in Dorset: The Prequel

Also available as an ebook

Table of Contents

The Three Steps ~ Write, Publish, Promote

So you want to write a memoir? People have said to you, "How interesting! You should write a book about your life!" You'd love to, and you have all these memories and stories churning about in your head, but you've never actually started...

Maybe you've kept journals, maybe you have photographs, but the thought of organising all that material into a book that people will actually want to read is terrifying.

How do you set about writing a memoir?

How do you get it published?

How do you market it?

I've written a series of successful memoirs. All my books quickly became Amazon bestsellers and I am proud to be a New York Times and Wall Street Journal bestselling author. I now feel ready and well-equipped to pass on all my secrets.

I hope this little book spells it all out clearly. How to *write* a good book, particularly a memoir, and how to *publish* and *promote* it. I've included all the tips I've learned along the way and all the advice I wish I'd had at my fingertips when I first started out as a writer.

There has never been a better time to write and publish a book, thanks to the Indie revolution. We no longer need to depend on agents and traditional publishers to take on our books. We writers can do *everything* ourselves, and it isn't difficult.

However, even if you've written and published a sensational book, it's very easy for it to drown in the ocean of new books that are being published daily. When I last looked, Amazon offered about six million books for sale and 10,000 new ones were being published every month. I'm sure this number has seriously escalated now.

Scary.

Established authors will tell you that writing and publishing your book is the easy part. Getting it noticed is much harder.

This book will give you practical advice, not only on writing and publishing, but offers 50 sure-fire ways to promote your masterpiece and get it noticed.

Victoria Twead

STEP 1 ~ WRITING YOUR MEMOIR

Real Name or *nom de plume?*

Dozens of people have asked me whether they should write under a *nom de plume*. My advice is *yes*, unless you are some kind of celebrity, in which case your name will sell books.

If your book becomes a bestseller, do you really want your privacy compromised? Do you want to be accosted by well-meaning fans when you go grocery shopping? Do you want your family pestered? Signing autographs may seem glamorous at first, but how quickly will you tire of it?

Also, your memoir may expose intimate secrets which makes it a sensible idea to hide behind a *nom de plume*.

So, what name should you choose?

Try to pick both a first name and surname that begin with a letter near the beginning of the alphabet. If your books are ever displayed on bookstore shelves, having a name like Andrew Barnes will ensure yours will be one of the first books customers see as they scan the shelves looking for a good read. Likewise, with a name like Amy Atkins, you'll be near the top of any list that is ordered alphabetically while few people ever reach poor Xavier Winters. It's too late for me now, but I'd heed this advice if I were ever to change my name.

For memoir writers, the name itself doesn't really matter, except that a shorter one uses fewer characters - handy if you create a Twitter account in your author name.

When you've thought of a name, Google it. Check that no other authors have the same name.

Title Choice

Picking a strong title for your memoir is very important. Research shows that the shorter the title, the more memorable it is and the better it sells. Titles with three or four words are supposed to be the best.

I called my first book *Chickens, Mules and Two Old Fools*. Much too long, probably, but it quickly became an Amazon bestseller and has sold many thousands. So I guess you can break the rules. Readers have written to me telling me that the quirky title of *Chickens* was what attracted them in the first place, so a long title worked for me although I wouldn't recommend it.

Memoir writers are lucky because it's quite acceptable, even expected, to have a subtitle. Subtitles clarify and expand the main title of a book. A good example is the bestseller *Eat, Pray, Love: One Woman's Search for Everything Across Italy, India and Indonesia.* The main title is short and snappy, and the subtitle describes exactly what the book is about. This book has become so well known that most people now just refer to it as *Eat, Pray Love*. But the subtitle undoubtedly helped when it was first published.

When people use a search box on a book site, they will type in a few words to describe the book they are looking for. These are keywords. Include some keywords in your subtitle, and your book will pop up.

By the time I was writing my third book, I had learned an enormous amount. I discovered that it's helpful to squeeze some keywords into the subtitle, if you can.

For example, my third book, *Two Old Fools on a Camel ~ from Spain to Bahrain and Back Again*, will appear when anyone types in the keyword 'Bahrain'. I believe that keywords have been a huge help in getting my books found.

Another thing worth mentioning. Before finalising your title, Google it. Do any other published books already have that title, or something similar? If so, let it go, and think again. Be as original as you can.

Ready, Steady, Go!

Starting to write a book is pretty daunting, but I've learned ways to simplify the whole process.

My first piece of advice works for me every time. Get yourself a big, blank sheet of paper, the bigger the better. Use it in 'landscape' position and draw a horizontal line straight across the middle. This is your timeline.

Every book, whether a memoir, fiction, or children's story book, needs a shape, with a beginning, middle, and end. However, a memoir is best when it concentrates on a specific time-span.

Decide where your story is going to start. Don't feel you need to describe everything from birth, just choose an appropriate point where your story begins.

Decide where you are going to finish. Perhaps your story continues, but that's fine because you'll have enough material for a sequel. If readers liked your first book, they'll eagerly await your second.

On your blank sheet of paper, write a few words on the left side that will remind you where you are going to start the story, and on the right side, where you are going to conclude.

Now start jotting notes along the line, just a few words that'll remind you of the particular event you want to describe. Try to do it in chronological order, using boxes, dates, arrows, or whatever will help.

Jotting down all these ideas on a timeline will organise your thoughts. Refer to your journals, if you have them. Write 'pic of Great Aunt Elsa', for example, to remind you to add a particular photo at that point.

Your sheet of paper may end up looking messy and jumbled, but you will understand it perfectly. Now you have that all-important skeleton of your book.

Your timeline is invaluable. Keep adding to it as thoughts occur to you, or as you recall stuff you may want to include. I find mine is never quite finished, and I still add little scribbled notes to myself throughout the writing process.

You may not use everything you've jotted down, but your notes are now ordered and organised.

The Two Most Important Chapters

Your first and last chapters are crucial.

Amazon readers or any online retailer will judge your book by that first 'Look Inside' or preview. On the strength of those first few paragraphs, your potential customer will either buy your book or move on to something more compelling.

In a bookstore, readers will thumb through your book, and they will probably read the first page. If they aren't hooked, they'll put your book down and pick up another.

This means that your first chapter and opening paragraphs need to be honed to perfection. They need to hook your readers, draw them in, and leave them wanting more.

Your last chapter is equally important. This is the chapter where your readers will decide whether they want to leave a good review or a dreadful one. It is also the point where they talk to other people about the book they've just finished. After the last chapter, if they enjoyed it, they will look for more books by the same author.

Chapter Length

Chapters were invented for a reason: they give the reader a breathing space. Chapters allow readers to put the book down for a while, to think about what they've just read, or to go off and finish washing the car, or whatever.

However, you may want to flout this advice and use your chapter ending in a totally different way. (See the Creating a Page-Turner, page 12.)

Chapter lengths can vary from author to author, and there are no rules. You can include chapters of varying length in your book if you wish.

I try to keep my chapters to around 2,500 words, give or take a couple of hundred, and that works for me.

Telling the Truth

Memoirs are nonfiction, and perhaps you are betraying a trust if you don't base your writing on truth, although everybody's memory of a particular event will be different.

There are bestselling memoirs, like *Fragments* by Binjamin Wilomirski and *Three Cups of Tea* by Greg Mortenson and David Oliver Relin that hit the headlines when they were denounced as not being true at all.

However, there are some instances when you may need to use a little artistic licence. I believe it's permissible to exaggerate sometimes. For instance, if you are describing a road that is often noisy, make it even noisier, or deafening.

Also, you may need to shuffle events around chronologically, to prevent your story from becoming fragmented and disjointed. For instance, if I am describing Christmas, I may combine events that happened at Christmases several years apart to make it a better reading experience.

The same applies to characters. They may act in a certain way with sizable time lapses in between, but I often decide to condense the events and chop out the time between to assist the flow of the book.

Very occasionally, I will combine the character traits of several different people and write them as one person. If I didn't do this, I would need to introduce too many characters, making it difficult for readers to remember who was who.

Should you use characters' real names? Be careful. In my books, I have a mixture of real names and fake names. When I use the genuine names, I always check with owners to make sure they don't mind. I use fake names for everybody else to protect their privacy, and to avoid possible libel suits, of course.

Locations are another pitfall. I had the foresight to change the name of our village, and I'm ever-thankful that I did. When I first started writing my *Old Fools* series, I had absolutely no idea that my books would become so popular. I had no idea that people would Google our village and scour maps, searching for the place we made our home. I receive emails regularly from people who want directions and plan their holidays with the idea of visiting our Spanish village. Changing its name was a good decision.

Pace

There are many tricks of the trade to keep your readers interested. You, as a writer, will have a unique 'voice', but that isn't enough. You must become an expert in pace, manipulating how the reader will read your work.

- Here's a simple, probably obvious tip. If you are writing descriptive passages, use longer sentences. If you are writing a harrowing scene, or trying to create tension, use short, sharp sentences.

- The best piece of writing advice I ever picked up was 'make every word count'. Apply this to every sentence you write. For instance, consider this sentence:

I was looking at him intently.

Now hone it down, and the rewritten version becomes:

I stared at him.

It's shorter, sharper and, I think you'll agree, has much more impact.

Here's another example:

Jane ran as quickly as she could to the edge of the green field.

Jane sprinted to the edge of the field.

Be sparing with those adverbs; you rarely need them because our language is so rich. There is invariably a much better word that you can choose instead. Adjectives and adverbs tend to slow the pace and may annoy the reader.

- Keep paragraphs short. Most of your readers will be reading on an e-reading device, like a Kindle, or even an iPhone. An overly long paragraph will fill the screen and is not a pleasant reading experience.

Creating a Page-Turner

This is actually easier than it sounds, although it goes against the advice I gave in the Chapter Length section, on page 9.

When writing a memoir, it is tempting to relate events and round them off at the end of the chapter. For instance, when describing a fishing trip where Grandpa fell into the water and nearly got eaten by a great white shark, you will probably finish the chapter by explaining how you fished Grandpa out just in time, and went home.

Instead, consider finishing your chapter at the point where Grandpa fell overboard and readers will feel compelled to turn the page to the next chapter to find out what happens next.

You don't need to use this device every time, but it will add excitement to your book.

Make sure that you recap a little in your following chapter to refresh the memories of readers who may have set the book aside for a while at the end of the last chapter.

Dialogue

Thumb through any copy of Harry Potter and you will discover that 70% of it is dialogue. This is no accident. Dialogue is easy to read and increases the pace. I wouldn't suggest such a heavy percentage for memoirs, but do ensure you include plenty of dialogue. It will inject life into your writing.

Good dialogue is the perfect tool to build characters and develop them. Allow character traits to show through your characters' spoken words. Think how characters choose their words and how this choice makes them unique, different from any other person in the world.

We have one particular friend who is posh, and when I write about her, I make her use words like 'spiffing' and 'awfully'. Even without adding a tag line, readers know exactly who is speaking.

Tag lines, or who says what and how they say it, are my pet hate. Take a look at these appalling examples:

"B-b-but why not?" he stuttered.

It's very clear that he is stuttering from the dialogue. The tag line *he stuttered* is unnecessary.

"HURRY UP!" she shouted impatiently.

We can see at a glance that the speaker is shouting because the words are written in upper case. The shouting, combined with the exclamation mark, shows us that she is impatient. Therefore, there is no need for *she shouted impatiently,* which can be deleted.

Don't be tempted to write dialogue in a dialect that is difficult to understand. If it is too hard to decipher, the reader will become frustrated.

As you write your dialogue, read it back to yourself, aloud. Ask yourself, does this sound natural? If not, rewrite.

Finally, should one use double or single quotation marks to denote speech? Both are right, so you decide. I like the old-fashioned double, but others don't. If you choose one type for dialogue, make sure you use the other for quotations. (British English.) For example:

"Serves you right! The sign said 'Do not touch' very clearly."

More Dialogue Tips

Some writers find it difficult to punctuate dialogue correctly.

Use the following models as examples of correctly punctuated dialogue. Note that the punctuation always falls *inside* speech marks.

"There's a fly in my soup."

or

"There's a fly in my soup," said Joe. "I believe it's doing the breast-stroke."

or

"There's a fly in my soup," said Joe, "and it's floating on its back."

or

Joe asked, "Is there a fly in my soup?"

In case you need reminding, make sure you start a new paragraph for each new speaker.

Vocabulary

Keeping your vocabulary rich and varied is essential, and a thesaurus should be your best friend.

Just to illustrate this point, I looked up the simple word 'walk', and my online thesaurus offered me the following alternatives:

advance, amble, ambulate, canter, escort, exercise, file, foot, go, go on foot, hike, hit the road, hoof it, knock about, lead, leg it, locomote, lumber, march, meander, pace, pad, parade, patrol, perambulate, plod, prance, promenade, race, roam, rove, run, saunter, scuff, shamble, shuffle, slog, stalk, step, stride, stroll, strut, stump, take a walk, toddle, tour, traipse, tramp, travel on foot, traverse, tread, trek, troop, trudge, wander, wend one's way

Of course, don't overdo it, or you'll appear as though you've swallowed a dictionary.

Never try to be too clever by using unfamiliar words. If readers don't understand the words you choose, however correct your choice may be, they'll be irritated.

Repetition

Even the best, most experienced writers may be unaware that they have favourite phrases that they often repeat. For instance, I can't help noticing how often Lee Child uses the phrase 'in a beat'. Happily, there is a quick cure.

Simply copy your chapters and paste them into an online 'Phrase Frequency Counter' like this one.

http://www.writewords.org.uk/phrase_count.asp

It will tell you instantly if you tend to repeat phrases. If you are guilty of the crime, you can then go back and edit the overused phrases.

I do this with all my books and am always horrified at the result. In the first draft of *Chickens, Mules and Two Old Fools,* I had written 'half an hour' twenty-three times...

Proofreading

Proofreading means searching for errors in grammar, spelling, spacing, punctuation, word choice, tense and organisation.

Of course you must proofread your own work, but that isn't enough. As the author, you will be blind to some mistakes because you will read what you expect to read, not what is actually written.

A helpful trick is to temporarily change your font and size to give it a different look.

It also helps enormously to print out your work, as you'll see it with slightly different eyes. Borrow the professional proofreader trick of using a ruler and checking line by line. The ruler forces you to focus on that line and doesn't allow your eye to stray.

Use your online proofreader and spellchecker, but bear in mind they won't find every typo. They won't pick out errors like writing 'loose' instead of 'lose'. Or missing the 't' out of 'the'. Only human eyes can spot that.

Friends and family can really help out at this stage. Get as many different people to proofread your manuscript (MS) as possible. This will help eliminate any errors that have slipped through.

In addition to my own books, I have a team who publish other authors' works under the name of Ant Press. We have trained proofreaders and never publish until we have proofread every manuscript, which we offer free of charge as part of our service.

However, although we are experienced proofreaders, I always pay to have my own books independently proofread. I am often horrified by the number of typos that are found by the professional when I thought I'd checked every word meticulously.

So, if at all possible, get your MS professionally proofed.

I can highly recommend Mindy Sampson, (US) or Zoe Marr (British, living in New Zealand) who proofread and copyedited several of my books. They are both marvels and can be contacted at:
Mindy: *mindymae@earthlink.net*

Zoe: zlmproof@gmail.com Website: http://www.zlmproofreading.com/

Finally, take comfort in the fact that typos still appear in even the most professional, traditionally published books.

Editing

Editing is not the same as proofreading. Editing is the ironing out of errors in the plot, character development, pace, structure, storyline, and tone.

When you have finished your final chapter, set the MS aside. Leave it for several days, longer if possible. Then read it again with fresh eyes. You'll be astonished at how many errors you'll pick out.

At this point, the most useful exercise you can do is to have a friend or family member read your work *aloud* to you. If there is nobody available, even reading it aloud to yourself is better than nothing.

Listening to your story read to you will help you pick out character inconsistencies or weaknesses in the plot.

Also, does the reader stumble at all? If so, rewrite that section so it flows better.

Of course, if you can afford it, get your editing done professionally.

I highly recommend joining a writers' circle, whether online or in your locality. New eyes, more brutally honest than your friends' and family's, will critique your work and give you valuable feedback. In exchange, you will read chapters of their work and voice your opinion on their writing efforts.

YouWriteOn.com is an excellent online writing community whose members come from all over the world. It's sponsored by the British Arts Council and highly respected. It's free to join and incredibly useful.

Fellow members will award you stars for different aspects of your writing, like characterisation, plot, pace, structure, and your use of language.

If you score high and reach the top five, you will win a free professional critique from a big publishing house or literary agent, who may take you on.

Size Matters

How long should a memoir be? That is a common question fired at me. There are no hard and fast rules, simply what readers expect when they buy a memoir. Feedback shows that readers feel a little cheated and complain when a memoir is less than 50,000 words, the size of a novella, or children's book.

However, anything over 110,000 words is considered too long and daunting. Consider too, the printing costs. If your book is going to be produced as a hardback or paperback, the extra pages will make it more expensive and perhaps discourage purchasers.

Somewhere between 75,000 and 95,000 words is probably ideal.

STEP 2 ~ PUBLISHING

Decisions

So now you have a finished manuscript and big decisions to make. The publishing world has exploded. Today you are free to choose either the traditional or self-publishing route. There are even hybrids.

No longer do you need to hawk your baby to literary agents and publishing houses, waiting months for an answer, if they bother to answer at all. Now your book can be displayed alongside titles from traditionally published authors, at least online.

When I finished my first book, *Chickens, Mules and Two Old Fools*, I sent query letters to agents and publishers. They all claimed they liked it, even loved it, but didn't think they'd be able to find a market for it.

Thank goodness I didn't give up at that point. I decided to self-publish and have sold many thousands of copies and ecopies of my books since then. Enough to make a living out of writing. In spite of those agents' lack of confidence in me, my series of memoirs are bestsellers, and I am a NYT and Wall Street Journal bestselling author. I am proof that you *can* succeed without a traditional contract.

Whether you take the traditional or self-publishing route, there are advantages and disadvantages with both which I have set out in the following sections.

The Traditional Route

If your memoir is published traditionally, the publishing house will proofread and edit your MS. They will design your cover and put your book up for sale in bricks-and-mortar bookstores. They will also convert and sell your book as an ebook.

If a traditional publisher takes you on, they will pay you an advance, and then royalties as your book sells. An 'advance' means exactly that; it refers to the money authors are paid ahead of time for their books. Perhaps it should be called 'advance against future earnings', because it represents money the publishing house is laying out that it has not yet made. As books are sold, you will start earning only when that advance figure has been reached.

You will be paid twice yearly, and your agent (if you have one) will also take his cut, probably around 15% of your royalties.

The biggest advantage of being published traditionally is that your book may be displayed in bricks-and-mortar bookstores, which is more difficult for self-publishers to accomplish. However, they won't get pride-of-place displays (e.g. window, eye-level shelves, central counter) unless your publisher pays extra. A big publisher will market your book, up to a point, arrange book-signing tours and advertising. However, you will also be expected to self-promote, using social media and other means.

The biggest disadvantage is that you will earn far less for each copy sold. After the publisher and agent have taken their cuts, your royalties will be a fraction of what you can earn as a self-published author. Unless you write many bestselling books, it is unlikely that you'll ever be able to give up the day job.

Always remember that you are losing most of your rights when you sign up with a traditional publisher.

Another disadvantage is that your publisher may change your book in ways you don't really approve of, so you should prepare yourself for that.

The Traditional Route - Agents and Query Letters

To be traditionally published, you will need to track down literary agents who handle memoirs, because very few traditional publishing houses accept unsolicited manuscripts.

You need to craft your query letter and your synopsis. There is plenty of online help to be found, or, if you live in the UK, buy the latest edition of 'The Writers and Artists Yearbook' which is a superb reference tool. Even established authors recommend the W&A Yearbook. *"Full of useful stuff. It answered my every question." --JK Rowling*

Your query letter to literary agents should consist of just three paragraphs on no more than one page.

1. The first paragraph is your 'hook', which should intrigue the agent. The conventional way is to start with the word 'When' and write in the third person, even though you are referring to yourself. The following example is the one I would use now for *Chickens, Mules and Two Old Fools* if I were sending out query letters to agents.

When Joe and Victoria relocate to a tiny, mountain village in Andalucía, they have no idea of the culture shock in store. No idea they'll become reluctant chicken farmers and own the most dangerous cockerel in Spain. No idea they'll help capture a vulture or be rescued by a mule. Will they stay, or return to the relative sanity of England?

2. The second paragraph is a mini-synopsis of your memoir. Somehow, you must condense your memoir into one short paragraph. This is a mini-synopsis I might use for my second book.

In my second memoir, 'Two Old Fools - Olé!', Joe and I have finished fixing up our house and look forward to peaceful days enjoying our retirement. Then the fish van arrives, and instead of delivering fresh fish, disgorges the Ufarte family. The peace of our tiny Spanish mountain village is shattered.

3. The third paragraph is your bio. Keep it short. Have you won any writing awards? Been published before? Don't include anything irrelevant, like past careers; only mention stuff related to your book, or what experiences you have had that resulted in your writing this memoir.

Finish your query letter by thanking the agent for his time and mentioning that you can provide the full manuscript upon request.

If a partial or full manuscript is requested, ensure that you follow these conventions, whether you are submitting your physical manuscript by mail or as a file via email.

- Your MS should be double spaced, with 1.0 inch to 1.25 inch margins all around. Use 12 point Times New Roman font.
- Page numbers should be inserted in the upper right-hand corner.
- Your author last name and abbreviated title should appear in the upper left corner on every page of your masterpiece. For example: Twead/Chickens
- Your cover sheet should list your contact information, the word count of your book, the book title, and your name.
- Your manuscript's title page should have your name, address, phone number, and email address listed on separate lines in the upper left corner of your title page.
- Each new chapter should start on a fresh page. The first paragraph should begin one-third down from the top of the page.
- Never staple your pages together.

If an agent takes you on, he will pitch your manuscript to publishing houses he thinks are a good fit for your work.

It has always been difficult to escape the slush pile. This is the name given to unsolicited query letters or manuscripts sent by authors, either directly to the publisher or literary agent. Sifting through the slush pile is a job often given to assistants or to outside readers. Your letter or MS could languish there for a long time.

Take heart in knowing that Beatrix Potter, Harper Lee, H.G. Wells, J.K. Rowling and many other famous writers were repeatedly rejected before being accepted.

The Self-Publishing Route

As with the traditional route, there are advantages and disadvantages if you decide to self-publish.

One huge advantage is that you will earn far more per book sold. You can choose your own price and can tinker with that until you reach the magic price point at which it seems to sell best.

It is also advantageous that, as a self-publisher, all rights remain your own and you are completely in charge of your book's destiny.

A disadvantage is that you will find it harder to persuade bricks-and-mortar bookstores to stock your paperback. Why should they take a book from an unknown author when traditional publishing houses supply them with a constant stream of, for example, celebrity memoirs?

As a self-published author, the responsibility of marketing your book usually rests entirely on your shoulders. However, if you are wise, you will find an independent publisher who specialises in memoirs and already has a healthy following of readers who love memoirs. That way, you can retain all your rights, get a head start on marketing and keep the majority of your earnings.

Self-Publishing (DIY)

Paperbacks

If you are happy to set up your own paperback, CreateSpace or Lulu are probably your best options. They print on demand (POD) and there is no need for an extended, expensive print run.

You will need to learn about trim sizes, bleed, embedding fonts, margins, copyright pages, submitting your book files, plus other terms and processes. It's free, but there is quite a steep learning curve. It's not difficult, but setting up the book can be daunting as it is fiddly and time-consuming.

You will be offered 'extended distribution' which means your book will appear on the major catalogues which supply stores like Barnes and Noble, and also libraries and academic institutions.

Ebooks

I was lucky because my first memoir, *Chickens, Mules and Two Old Fools*, was published at the very start of the ebook revolution, back in 2009. It was a steep learning curve, but Joe and I taught ourselves how to convert my MS into all the different ebook formats required by different ereading devices.

Ebooks are very different animals from physical books. Ebooks flow seamlessly from page to page, depending on which ereader device the reader is using. An ebook needs to look just as attractive on a tiny iPhone screen as it does on an iPad or Kindle. An ebook needs an interactive table of contents. Each new chapter must begin on a new page. You cannot choose the font your ebook is formatted in; the reader selects that for himself.

In the beginning, our efforts weren't pretty, but gradually Joe and I taught ourselves how to make my ebooks a smooth, pleasant reading experience, and how to add photographs and recipes. We experimented with all the software available and kept abreast of the ever-changing modification demands.

Now, not only do we produce our own ebooks, but we convert and publish other authors' books, under the Ant Press imprint.

How to construct an ebook from scratch is outside the scope of this handbook as it's quite a technical process. However, there is a wealth of free information on the Internet that will steer you through the process if you are happy to learn.

Self-Publishing (Conversion Services)

Ebooks

Converting your MS into an ebook is quite technical and you may not want to attempt it.

However, there are some reputable companies and individuals who will convert your MS to an ebook, starting from as little as £20 ($30). They may charge more if images are included.

They will hand you the finished product in .mobi (for Amazon Kindle) .epub (for most other ereading devices) and PDF for those wishing to read on their computer screens.

This is good. However, if you need to make corrections or changes, (and, believe me, everyone does, often...) or insert additional material, such as mentioning a new book, this will incur further charges.

You will now need to upload your newly converted .epub and .mobi files to all the different online selling platforms, unless you opt for the Amazon

Select program which insists on exclusivity. If you are in Select, you can *only* sell on Amazon.

Some online retailers require International Standard Book Numbers (ISBNs) which your conversion service will not provide. Amazon (which uses its own identification number or ASIN) and a few others, do not require ISBNs. You can upload without one, and therefore you won't need to buy an ISBN for those companies.

An ISBN is a unique 10 or 13 digit number product identifier used by publishers, booksellers, libraries and Internet retailers for ordering, listing, sales records and stock control purposes. You must purchase your own unique ISBN from your own country.

Buying single ISBNs is not practical and will cost you almost as much as buying ten. In the UK, Nielsen will charge you £126 for ten ISBNs. A block of ten ISBNs from Bowker in the USA will cost $250. ISBNs are issued free of charge in Canada.

Bear in mind that your conversion service will not undertake any promotion or marketing for you; they are purely a conversion service.

Self-Publishing (Vanity Press)

Thousands of publishers have sprung up from nowhere and will charge a hefty fee to publish your book in paperback and to have your book converted to an ebook. This is called 'vanity' printing.

In addition to charging you in advance, vanity presses will deduct a percentage from every sale.

When I first started out as a writer, I made expensive mistakes. I paid to have my paperbacks published. I have since learned that there is absolutely no need for this. In my opinion, YOU SHOULD PAY NOTHING to have your book published, either as a paperback or ebook.

I was horrified to receive an email from an author who was on the point of parting with well over £1,000 (about $1,535) to have his book published. I was delighted to be able to tell him that there are plenty of independent publishers available (see next chapter) who would do the same, or a better job, free of charge.

Beware! When choosing a company to produce your book, watch for any of the following danger signals:

✗ They will charge you money for publishing your paperback.

✗ They will accept any book, regardless of quality or genre.

✗ You will be expected to format your paperback yourself and upload it to their website.

✗ If you don't already have a cover designed, they will offer you a choice of readymade ones, just inserting your title and author name.

✗ They either don't edit, or charge extra for editing and proofreading.

✗ They offer no proper help with promotion, unless you pay for an expensive marketing package.

✗ They are difficult to contact and slow to answer emails.

Self-Publishing (Independent Presses)

Perhaps I'm biased, but this is the solution I recommend. However, beware, as not all companies offer the same benefits.

Find an independent publisher who specialises in your genre, and check these points:

✓ Are they free of charge? (If they charge the author, they are vanity presses.)

✓ Look at their website very carefully. Are their terms clearly spelled out?

✓ Do they specialise in your genre?

✓ Are they selective, not accepting every submitted MS regardless of quality?

✓ Will they produce both the paperback and ebook?

✓ Do they proofread and edit at no extra charge?

✓ Do they help market and promote? If so, how?

✓ Do they have a healthy, ready-made following of readers?

✓ Will you be given your own author page on their website, with links taking customers straight to retailers?

✓ Do they have their own Facebook page?

✓ Will they work with you to come up with a good cover design?

✓ How long will you be tied to this publisher? If it's for more than 2 years, beware.

✓ Will they upload your memoir ebook to all the major selling platforms, such as all of Amazon's territories, Kobo, iBooks, Nook and Diesel, unless you opt for Amazon Select?

✓ Are they friendly and accessible?

✓ Do they provide free ISBNs?

✓ Do they pay monthly and give a breakdown of how many of your books were sold, and where?

✓ Are you free to sell the translation rights to your book, if approached?

✓ Has this company already published any bestsellers?

✓ Contact some authors already published by this company. Were they happy with the service?

I'm happy to say that Ant Press can answer positively to all these questions, but there are plenty of other companies around that will do an equally good job. Consider a company that somebody has recommended to you. Shop around!

(This is how it works at Ant Press. We charge nothing, but keep a small percentage of royalties. This means that Ant Press and similar companies are just as keen as you are to sell as many of your books as possible and catapult them to bestseller status.)

Note: It is also worth mentioning 'aggregators' at this point. These are organisations who will convert your memoir into an ebook, issue you with free ISBNs and upload it for you to different online selling platforms. For this they will take 15% of your royalties. They do not proofread or edit and give no individual promotion assistance. The major players are Smashwords and Draft2Digital.

At Smashwords, you are required to put your carefully formatted Word doc through their 'meatgrinder' which can be a painful and lengthy process, often taking many attempts before it is accepted.

Draft2Digital have made the process much easier but do not upload to many retailers yet, but are growing fast.

The Front Cover

Whether you intend to self-publish your memoir as a paperback or an ebook, you will need a stunning, high-resolution cover design. If you intend to design your own, here are some basic rules.

Both Paperback and Ebook

- The background colour chosen should never be white, because most book retail sites have white backgrounds and your book will not show up.
- Use a large, plain, easy-to-read font for the title of your book so that it can still be read, even as a tiny icon.
- Don't use too many different fonts or font colours because the finished cover will look cheap and jumbled.
- Keep your design simple for maximum impact. Shrink it to thumbnail size and ask an unbiased person who has never seen it before to offer an opinion.
- Consider having your cover designed professionally. Prices will vary hugely, so shop around.

Paperback only

- Decide what size you want your paperback to be. The industry standards are 9 x 6 and 5 x 8 and it's best to stick with those so that your books will fit on bookshelves neatly.
- To include the back cover and spine, you will need an all-in-one design that wraps around.
- Go to a cover generator, such as the one at *LightningSource.com*. Type in your details, including paper preference for the interior of your book (white or cream) and page count. Both will affect the spine width. A template will then be generated to your exact requirements. Use this template (it'll be a pdf or Photoshop compatible file) to lay out your design. (See the next chapter for back cover tips.)
- Your finished design should be saved as a pdf and a jpg with at least 300dpi.

Ebook only

- For online retailers such as Amazon and Apple iBooks, the dimensions should be at least 1,600 pixels x 2,400 pixels. (Height is 33% greater than width)
- The high resolution version (300dpi) will be the one you upload to retail sites, but it's good to save your file in low resolution in varying sizes for uploading onto websites and online promotion opportunities.

The Back Cover

Paperback

A paperback needs a good back cover design. On the back cover, pride of place should be given to your 'blurb', the teaser that will hook your potential reader. This may be the same as the one you used when writing query letters to agents, and your product description on Amazon.

The back cover blurb should be kept short. Potential buyers are browsing books at this point, and they won't bother to read long, involved blurbs. Unless they are hooked by the first couple of sentences, they will move on, and you will have lost the sale.

Take a look at some bestsellers on the market and learn from the way their blurbs are written.

The rules are:

- Write in the third person.
- Don't attempt to go into too much detail.
- Set the scene.
- Whet the reader's appetite.

This is the blurb from my third book, which hit the NYT bestseller list and has sold many thousands of copies.

"When Vicky and Joe reluctantly leave their Spanish mountain village to work in the Middle East, how could they know that the Arab revolution was poised to erupt, throwing them into violent events that would make world headlines?

Teaching Arab kids, working with crazy teachers, forming life-long friendships and being placed under house arrest, Vicky and Joe laugh and lurch through their year in Bahrain."

The back cover is also the perfect place to include a few quotes of praise. Do you know anyone famous who might give you a sentence? Can you quote a few words from reviewers?

If you have any writing awards, mention them.

If you are designing your own cover, don't forget to leave space for the ISBN at the bottom.

Ebook

An ebook doesn't require a back cover.

Front Matter

This is the stuff that appears before the first chapter. There are slightly different conventions between paperback and ebook.

Paperback

Page 1: Title, Subtitle (optional), Author.

Page 2: Copyright notice.

Example:

Copyright © Text Victoria Twead, 2013

Copyright © Photographs Victoria Twead, 2013

Produced by Ant Press

First Edition

The author asserts the moral right under the Copyright, Designs and Patents Act 1988 to be identified as the author of this work.

All rights reserved. No part of this publication may be reproduced, stored in a retrieval system, or transmitted, in any form or by any means without the prior written consent of the author, nor be otherwise circulated in any form of binding or cover other than that in which it is published and without a similar condition being imposed on the subsequent purchaser.

Page 3: Author bio and photo (optional and can be included on page 1 if you prefer, or included at the back of your book, or not at all).

Page 4: Acknowledgments (optional). Whom do you need to thank? Have you quoted anybody? Do you want to mention anybody?

Page 5: Dedication (optional).

Page 6: Table of Contents (TOC).

Page 7: Chapter 1. However you choose to set out your front matter, the first chapter MUST begin on an ODD page in a paperback. Page numbering also begins at this point.

Ebook

There is a very good reason for keeping your front matter short and simple in an ebook. The 'preview' or 'Look Inside' option for browsers usually allows 10% - 20% of your book to be visible. You want the reader to be able to access your opening chapters, not just the front matter. Authors nowadays have begun to put their copyright notice and acknowledgments at the back, instead of the front.

Page 1: Title, Subtitle, Author, Copyright (summary only).

Page 2: Dedication (optional)

Page 3: Table of Contents

Page 4: Chapter 1

TOC (Table of Contents)

Paperback

If you are formatting your own paperback, keep your TOC very neat and well aligned.

Although you'll use single spacing for the main body of your memoir, the TOC is often easier to read when double spaced.

Check, double check and check again that your page numbers are correct. This is one of the last jobs to do before submitting your book for publishing.

Ebook

For an ebook, your TOC needs to be interactive. Any reader using their Kindle, Nook or iPad should be able to tap on a chapter title in the TOC and be sent straight to that location. As with the paperback TOC, space it wider than you would the main body of the memoir. Remember, your chapter headings are live, and if you squeeze them too close together you will end up with a virtual 'minefield'. Chubby fingers will find it difficult to tap the intended links.

Fonts

Paperback

If you are preparing your own paperback for publication, you can't go far wrong with Times New Roman (TNR) 11pt. It's easy to read, unobtrusive, classic and elegant. Remember, it's your words you want people to concentrate on, not your font.

However, if you think TNR is too common or boring, you could choose from:

Cambria

Hoefler

Garamond

Century

Minion Pro

Georgia

Don't forget that your choice of font will affect the number of pages in your paperback. Some fonts are wider than others. The less pages your book has, the less expensive it will be to print.

Here is the same line of writing in different fonts, all Regular, size 11:

TNR	Abcde fghi-Jkl mn. "Opq!" Rstuv w xyz.
Cambria	Abcde fghi-Jkl mn. "Opq!" Rstuv w xyz.
Hoefler	Abcde fghi-Jkl mn. "Opq!" Rstuv w xyz.
Garamond	Abcde fghi-Jkl mn. "Opq!" Rstuv w xyz.
Century	Abcde fghi-Jkl mn. "Opq!" Rstuv w xyz.
Minion Pro	Abcde fghi-Jkl mn. "Opq!" Rstuv w xyz.
Georgia	Abcde fghi-Jkl mn. "Opq!" Rstuv w xyz.

Ebook

You have no choice of fonts when constructing an ebook. Simply use Times New Roman 12pt, or similar, as the reader will choose his own preferred font on his ereader. The reader will also adjust the font size to suit himself.

Indentation

Paperback and Ebook

For memoirs and fiction, the first line of a paragraph is usually indented (0.25in) except for the very first line at the beginning of a chapter, after a chapter head. That first line should have no indent, and neither should the first line after a scene break.

Reference books, like this one, use the 'block' paragraph, which is not indented, but has a space between paragraphs.

Scene Breaks

Paperback and Ebook

To divide scenes, scene break symbols are used. A rule that flower-arrangers already know: always use an odd, not an even amount, as it is more pleasing to the eye. Be as original as you like by exploring the Special Characters offered by your word-processing program. For my book, *Two Old Fools on a Camel*, (set in the Middle East) I chose to repeat a letter of the Arabic alphabet.

ش ش ش

You can even use jpgs repeated in a row. In my first book, *Chickens, Mules and Two Old Fools*, I used little Rainbow Men, as they are the emblem for the part of Spain I was writing about.

𝍓 𝍓 𝍓

If you prefer, just use centrally aligned asterisks.

*****

Page Numbering

Paperback

When preparing your MS for publishing as a paperback, you will need to insert page numbers. These are best placed at the bottom, in the centre, font size 9 or 10. You can use the 'footer' facility in your word-processor for this.

The title pages and first pages should show no page numbers. Your numbering should begin at your first chapter and begin with 5, or whatever page number your first chapter falls on, not 1.

Your total page count MUST be divisible by two, and your last page should be totally blank. Do NOT number your blank page. A barcode will be inserted on your very last page by the printers.

Ebook

When preparing a book for ebook conversion, you can ignore page numbering completely. Ereaders do not use page numbers but show 'locations' instead. These are set automatically, and you have no control.

Chapter Heads

Paperback

In a paperback, your first chapter must begin on an odd page. It doesn't matter if subsequent chapters begin on an odd or even page, but of course each new chapter must start on a *fresh* page.

The chapter heading (sometimes referred to as the chapter title or chapter head) should be set lower down on the page, leaving blank space above.

Your chapter title or heading should be in a slighter larger size font than the body text, and is usually bold. You can choose whether you prefer chapter heads to be left aligned or centered.

Ebook

New chapters in ebooks should also start on a fresh 'page', but you don't need to concern yourself with odd or even pages as they don't exist in ebooks.

Formatting chapter heads for ebooks is the same as for paperbacks: use a slightly bigger font size, in bold, and either centered or left aligned.

Back Matter

This is the stuff that appears after the last chapter.

Paperback

The end of a paperback is a good place to include a list of other books you may have written. Add an excerpt to whet the reader's appetite. If this is your first book, but you have another planned, mention that there will be a sequel.

Add a sentence like:

Victoria Twead is currently working on a sequel to this book. If you would like to be informed when the sequel is published, please contact her by email.

TopHen@VictoriaTwead.com

If you didn't include About the Author in your front matter, you can do so here. (See example below.)

Add some contact links, such as your website, Facebook page and Twitter address.

Ebook

Unlike the paperback, the end of an ebook is the best place to put Other Books by the Author, Acknowledgments, About the Author, Contacts and Links and finally, your Copyright Notice.

Other Books by the Author: Have you written other books? If so, make sure you've listed them with live links to take the customer straight to them.

If you haven't written any other books, but have one planned, mention that there will be a sequel. Add a sentence like, *If you would like to be notified when the sequel is published, please contact the author at TopHen@VictoriaTwead.com*

Collect the email addresses in a list and make sure you contact them when your sequel is published.

If you have written a sequel, consider including the first chapter, or an excerpt, as a preview.

Acknowledgments: This is a list of people you are thanking, and the reason why. It may be people who helped you write your memoir, or places that gave you information you needed.

About the Author: Add an author photograph (optional), followed by a brief bio (no more than 100 words). Write it in the third person and keep it light; this is not a résumé. You will see mine at the end of this book.

Contact and Links: It is important to include an email address your readers can use to contact you, even if you have mentioned it before.

This is crucial because memoirs trigger emotions in readers and, having just finished your book, they will be eager to contact you. Answer every single email, which is only good manners since they've taken the trouble to write to you.

Include your website address if you have one.

If you have Twitter and Facebook accounts, list these links and make them clickable. Always respond when people contact you.

Often there are all sorts of photographs that you weren't able to include in your memoir. *Pinterest.com* gives you the perfect opportunity to display those photos to the world. Make sure you include a link to your Pinterest board at the end of the book.

Copyright Notice: Simply copy the following.

Copyright Notice

STEP 3 ~ 50 PROMOTION TIPS

If you thought writing and publishing was arduous, you may find promotion even tougher! It's never-ending, but essential to get your book noticed in the tsunami of new books flooding the market. Try to set aside a little time every day for marketing and you will reap the rewards.

Here is a list of promotion ideas, in no particular order.

1. As soon as your memoir is finished, offer free review copies to anybody who might be interested. Reviews are your very best selling tool.

2. Create an attractive website and keep it updated. Include your book cover, a sample chapter, author headshot, review snippets and links to retailers. Don't forget to add contact details.

3. Start a blog and allow people to interact. The more comments you receive, the busier your website will become, and the higher it will rise on Google searches.

4. Welcome guest blog posts and become a guest blogger yourself on other people's sites.

5. Interview other memoir authors and offer yourself for interviews.

6. Make yourself easily available on Facebook. Do not underestimate the power of Facebook: it is extremely useful if used correctly. I'm not one of those who constantly mentions my books on Facebook, although there are many writers who are happy to keep pushing their titles, and it seems to work for them. I prefer to chat about general, everyday stuff and have made some fantastic friends on Facebook. If people like you they'll probably buy your books.

7. Make a Facebook Fan Page. I have one, but don't use it very much because blatant self-promotion makes me uncomfortable. However, other authors use theirs to great effect, posting up good reviews and any other book news.

8. Create Facebook events, like competitions, and invite people to them.

9. Answer every single comment made to you on Facebook, or 'Like' it to acknowledge you've seen it.

10. Open a Twitter account and follow back anybody who follows you. Don't spam constantly but rather engage in conversations and your following will increase.

11. Join Pinterest and start a board for your book. Pin up your cover, author picture and any relevant photos you may have.

12. Join Google+ and host Q & A sessions.

13. Search for relevant forums on the Internet. I joined expat forums and chicken forums even before *Chickens, Mules and Two Old Fools* was published, and made many friends there who probably bought my books. Whatever your niche, be it sailing, mental health or transgender operations, forums will exist for you.

14. If you are a confident Internet user, create a 'Ning' community, or a forum of your own based on the theme of your book. It will attract potential purchasers of your book.

15. Join relevant Facebook groups.

16. Join Shelfari which is owned by Amazon. Put in all your book details and they will appear on readers' devices.

17. Join Goodreads, also owned by Amazon and become an active member. However, never self-promote except on the threads that invite authors to talk about their own books.

18. Join Librarything and add your book.

19. Consider giving away a few paperbacks or ecopies on the Librarything Giveaways in exchange for reviews. (Not if you are in the Amazon Select program.)

20. Visit your local bookstores. Offer to hold a book-signing event.

21. Ask local bookstores if they'll take a few copies of your book on sale or return. If they sell, the store will ask for more. If they don't, you can collect the books and you've lost nothing.

22. Contact local newspapers. They are usually happy to promote local authors.

23. Contact local radio stations. They are always looking for fresh content.

24. Contact online radio stations. Again, they are always looking for new people to interview.

25. Collect email addresses of anyone genuinely interested in your book and you'll be able to notify them when you write another.

26. Consider starting a monthly or bi-monthly newsletter for subscribers.

27. To build up your subscriber list, run a monthly drawing for a signed copy of your book. Announce the winners on Twitter, Facebook and your website.

28. Make business cards with your book cover on one side and contact details on the other. You'll be surprised how often the opportunity arises to hand them out. Get them professionally printed (Vistaprint is good and inexpensive). Don't attempt to print them off on a home printer.

29. Write articles for sites like Squidoo, Scribd and Ezine. Figure out which categories within these sites attract the same audience as your book, and write for those.

30. Write press releases. There is an art to this, so follow the proper format. Advice can be found in numerous places, such as *www.savvybookwriters.com* and *www.biblioscribe.com*

31. Submit your press releases to journalists and places like:
http://www.prlog.org/
http://www.1888pressrelease.com/
http://i-newswire.com/
http://www.prfocus.com/

32. Make a simple book trailer. It should be no more than two minutes long. Like your blurb, consider this as a 'teaser', and end it with links to your book. Add the book trailer to YouTube, Vimeo and your website and any retail sites that will allow it.

33. Join *Bookbuzzr.com* and *Freado.com*. Apart from the publicity, they offer a great book flipper widget you can add to your website or blog. (This is a tiny version of your book with turning pages.)

34. Include links to your book and website at the end of every email you send, as a signature.

35. Create flyers and leave them in places that attract your potential audience. Is your book about the horse world? Attend a horse event and hand out flyers.

36. Make bookmarks to give away. A cheap way of doing this is to print your design, repeated three times side by side, on an oversized postcard. (Vistaprint offers these postcards.) That way, 100 printed postcards will make 300 bookmarks. (Tax deductible expense.)

37. Invest in a magnetic sign that you can affix to your car. Every time you drive anywhere, you are advertising. (Tax deductible expense.)

38. Offer to take part in book club sessions via Skype.

39. Write up some discussion questions for book clubs. Either include them in the back of your book or on your website, or both.

40. Offer to attend local book clubs in person.

41. Offer to speak at your local Women's Institute or any clubs that welcome guest speakers.

42. Subscribe to Google Alerts. Google will then notify you automatically every time you or your book is mentioned on the Internet. Then you can thank those people, or join in the discussion.

43. Donate a couple of copies of your book to local libraries. If the book is popular, the library will keep replacing it as necessary. The average lifetime of a paperback in a library is 27 loans.

44. Create new fans by donating books (depending on your theme) to women's shelters, hospitals, retirement homes, local B&Bs, prisons or hospitals.

45. Donate your book to *Bookcrossing.com*

46. Set up a stall at a fete, flea market or car boot sale. Sell signed copies and give away bookmarks. Often it's not the number of books you sell that is most useful, but the contacts you make whilst chatting to people.

47. Rent a billboard.

48. Have some coffee mugs printed with your book cover and give them away.

49. Go to *Authorgraph.com* and set up an electronic autograph that owners of ebooks can request.

50. And finally, the very best way to sell books is to write another...

About the Author

In 2004 Victoria Twead left Britain and her teaching career behind to relocate to a tiny, remote mountain village in Andalucía. There she and Joe became reluctant chicken farmers and owned the most dangerous cockerel in Spain.

Village life inspired Victoria's *Old Fools* series, which has hit the New York Times and Wall Street Journal bestselling lists.

Victoria and Joe continue to enjoy life keeping chickens, writing, helping authors publish their books, sampling the local wine and living alongside their colourful neighbours.

Bestsellers by Victoria Twead

Chickens, Mules and Two Old Fools by Victoria Twead
(Wall Street Journal Top 10 bestseller)

Two Old Fools ~ Olé! by Victoria Twead

Two Old Fools on a Camel by Victoria Twead
(New York Times bestseller x 3)

Two Old Fools in Spain Again by Victoria Twead

One Young Fool in Dorset: The Prequel by Victoria Twead

Contacts and Links

Email:
TopHen@VictoriaTwead.com

Victoria's website:
www.VictoriaTwead.com

Free Stuff
http://www.victoriatwead.com/Free-stuff/

Victoria Twead on Facebook:
https://www.facebook.com/VictoriaTwead

Twitter:
@VictoriaTwead and *@StephenFrysCat*

Ant Press

Ant Press Website
www.AntPress.org

More Ant Press Bestselling Titles

Fat Dogs and French Estates ~ Part I by Beth Haslam

Fat Dogs and French Estates ~ Part II by Beth Haslam

Into Africa with 3 Kids, 13 Crates and a Husband by Ann Patras

Paw Prints in Oman: Dogs, Mogs and Me by Charlotte Smith
(New York Times bestseller)

The Coconut Chronicles: Two Guys, One Caribbean Dream House by
Patrick Youngblood

Joan's Descent into Alzheimer's by Jill Stoking

The Girl Behind the Painted Smile: My battle with the bottle
by Catherine Lockwood

Made in the USA
San Bernardino, CA
17 October 2017